ZANZI

TRAVEL

GUIDE 2024

Your Ultimate Companion for Adventure and
Relaxation. Discover the Best Beaches,
Cuisine,unforgettable Journeys,Hidden
Gems and Culture with Local Insights and
Pro Tips

Steven J. Chandler

TABLE OF CONTENTS

INTRODUCTION

Get ready for an amazing adventure in Zanzibar! It's like stepping into a magical place where the beautiful blue ocean meets a tapestry of interesting stories. Zanzibar is not just a regular spot on the map – it's an exciting invitation to discover hidden treasures and have special experiences.

Imagine sitting on the super clean beaches of Nungwi, feeling the warm sun, and listening to traditional music. This is the kind of place where every part has a story to tell, from the narrow streets in Stone Town to the sweet-smelling spice farms.

As you read through this guide, think of it like a friend telling you all about the coolest things in Zanzibar. You'll explore interesting places, taste yummy local food, and maybe even try some fun activities. It's not just a book with information; it's like a journey you take with a friend who knows all the best spots.

So, get ready to uncover the secrets of Zanzibar! Each page will take you on an adventure, showing you not just where to go, but also why it's so special. Your exciting journey in Zanzibar begins here, where dreams meet reality under the sunny African sky. Welcome to the wonderful world of Zanzibar – a place where every moment is a chance to discover, enjoy, and remember.

Why Visit Zanzibar?

A glimpse into why Zanzibar beckons travelers with its irresistible charm. In the heart of Stone Town, I found myself transported through time, surrounded by centuries-old architecture whispering stories of Swahili sultans, Arabian traders, and European explorers. The vibrant markets, where locals and visitors mingle through narrow streets, create an atmosphere where every step feels like a cultural exploration.

Beyond its historical allure, Zanzibar's charm lies in its diverse landscapes. Venture into the lush interiors of the islands, and you'll discover spice plantations, each leaf telling the aromatic legacy of Zanzibar's spice trade. The flavors of local cuisine, infused with the essence of cloves, cardamom, and cinnamon, offer a culinary journey that echoes the island's historical connections.

So, why should you visit Zanzibar? It's more than a destination; it's an immersive odyssey where the magic isn't confined to the glossy pages of a guidebook but comes to life in encounters with friendly locals, exploration of hidden gems, and the discovery of traditions that have withstood the test of time.

So as you delve into the pages of this comprehensive travel companion, envision yourself navigating the labyrinthine streets of Stone Town, where each cobblestone has a story to tell. Feel the soft embrace of the trade winds as you lounge on the pristine beaches of Nungwi or Paje. Immerse yourself in the vibrant culture that defines Zanzibar, from the rhythmic beats of traditional music to the intoxicating aromas of street food stalls.

This guide isn't just a compendium of information; it's a key to unlock the door to an extraordinary adventure. Each page unfolds a new facet of Zanzibar, offering insights into must-see attractions, accommodation options, culinary delights, and outdoor adventures that await your exploration. Your journey begins here, and with every turn of the page, let the anticipation of your own Zanzibar story unfurl.

CHAPTER 1

PLANNING YOUR TRIP

Welcome to the first step of your Zanzibar adventure! Planning is key to making your trip smooth and enjoyable. Let's dive into the details to ensure you're well-prepared for the journey ahead.

When to Visit

Zanzibar has great weather all year round, but knowing when to go can enhance your experience.

- **Ideal Seasons and Climate:** Learn about the different seasons in Zanzibar and what kind of weather to expect. This will help you decide when the best time for your visit is.
- **Special Events and Festivals:** Discover local celebrations happening during your stay. From lively festivals to cultural events, being part of these can add extra joy to your trip.

How to Get to Zanzibar

Getting to Zanzibar is exciting! Let's explore the various ways you can reach this beautiful destination.

- **Air Travel Options:** Find out about flights and airports. You'll be guided on the best routes and what to consider when booking your flight.
- **Seaport Information:** If you prefer the sea, you should locate a seaport and get info on ports and ferry services that can take you to Zanzibar.

Getting Around

Once you're on the islands, it's time to explore. Learn about the different ways you can move around Zanzibar.

- **Transportation within Zanzibar:** Discover options like taxis, rentals, and private transfers for comfortable island exploration.
- **Public Transport Options:** Dive into the local experience by using public transportation. It's not only budget-friendly but also a great way to connect with Zanzibar's culture.

What to Pack

Packing smartly ensures you have everything you need. Let's create a checklist and talk about what clothes to bring.

- **Essential Items Checklist:** Be guided on what documents and essentials to pack so you're ready for any adventure.
- **Clothing Recommendations:** Get tips on what to wear for various activities and occasions. Dress comfortably for the warm Zanzibar climate.

Entry and Visa Requirements

Understanding entry rules is crucial. Let's go through the visa process and what's required to enter Zanzibar smoothly.

- **Visa Application Process:** Step-by-step help on getting your visa, making sure you have all the necessary paperwork.
- **Entry Regulations:** Learn about the rules you need to follow when arriving in Zanzibar.

Currency and Language

Knowing about money and language is handy for a great experience in Zanzibar.

- **Local Currency Guide:** Understand the local money, exchange rates, and get tips on handling your finances during your stay.
- **Common Phrases in Swahili:** Study some basic Swahili phrases to help you communicate with the locals and make your experience even more special.

Visiting Zanzibar on a Budget

Traveling on a budget is possible and can lead to amazing adventures. Get ready for some smart tips and affordable activities.

- **Budget-Friendly Activities:** Explore activities that won't hurt your wallet but will give you a rich experience of Zanzibar.

Get excited about your Zanzibar journey! This chapter has all the details you need to plan your trip with confidence. Whether you're a seasoned traveler or a first-time explorer, we're here to make sure your Zanzibar adventure is off to a fantastic start!

CHAPTER 2

MUST-SEE ATTRACTIONS AND LANDMARKS

Embark on a journey through the heart of Zanzibar, where every step is a discovery and every landmark tells a story. In this chapter, we'll unravel the must-see attractions that make Zanzibar a captivating tapestry of history, nature, and culture.

Historical Sites

- Stone Town Exploration

Welcome to Stone Town, a living testament to Zanzibar's rich history. The narrow alleys, ancient buildings, and bustling markets create an immersive experience that transports you through time. As you wander through the labyrinthine streets, each weathered door whispers tales of Swahili sultans, Arabian traders, and European explorers.

Navigating the alleys of Stone Town felt like stepping into a living history book. The vibrant colors, the echoes of traditional music, and the aroma of spices created a sensory journey that etched Zanzibar's past into my memory.

- Spice Plantations

Venture into the lush interiors of Zanzibar to explore the spice plantations that have shaped the island's identity. Cloves, cardamom, cinnamon – the air is infused with the aromatic legacy of Zanzibar's spice trade. A guided tour reveals the cultivation process, allowing you to touch, smell, and taste the spices that have drawn traders and explorers for centuries.

Visiting a spice plantation was a sensory delight. Feeling the texture of fresh cloves, inhaling the sweet scent of vanilla, and savoring the taste of locally grown spices offered a deeper understanding of Zanzibar's cultural and economic history.

Natural Wonders

- Jozani Chwaka Bay National Park

For nature enthusiasts, Jozani Chwaka Bay National Park is a haven of biodiversity. The lush greenery is home to the rare red colobus monkeys, a species found only in Zanzibar. Stroll along the elevated boardwalks, allowing you to observe these playful creatures in their natural habitat while supporting conservation efforts.

Witnessing the red colobus monkeys leaping among the trees in Jozani Chwaka Bay National Park was a magical moment. The park's commitment to conservation and the chance to observe these unique primates up close made it a highlight of my Zanzibar adventure.

- Stunning Beaches

Zanzibar's coastline is adorned with pristine beaches, each offering a unique charm. Nungwi, with its powdery sands and vibrant nightlife, contrasts with the serene shores of Paje, where kite surfers dance with the wind. Whether you seek relaxation or water adventures, Zanzibar's beaches cater to every preference.

Spending a day at Nungwi Beach, where the turquoise waters meet golden sands, was pure bliss. The rhythmic sound of the waves, the warmth of the sun, and the vibrant energy of beach life created a perfect day in paradise.

Cultural Landmarks

- Old Fort and House of Wonders

Step into Zanzibar's cultural heart by exploring the Old Fort and the House of Wonders. The Old Fort, with its sturdy walls and historical significance, provides a glimpse into the island's resilience. Meanwhile, the House of Wonders stands as a majestic symbol of Zanzibar's cultural grandeur.

Standing within the walls of the Old Fort, I felt a connection to the past. The House of Wonders, illuminated at night, exuded a timeless elegance that encapsulated Zanzibar's cultural richness.

- Local Villages and Communities

To truly understand Zanzibar, venture beyond the tourist hubs to local villages and communities. Engage with the friendly locals, witness traditional practices, and immerse yourself in the authentic way of life that has endured for generations.

Exploring local villages introduced me to the warmth of Zanzibar's people. From participating in traditional dances to sharing stories with villagers, it was a cultural exchange that added depth to my Zanzibar experience.

Zanzibar's must-see attractions and landmarks are a captivating blend of history, nature, and culture. Each site narrates a unique story, creating an immersive experience for every traveler. Whether you're drawn to the historical charm of Stone Town, the natural wonders of Jozani Chwaka Bay, or the cultural richness of local villages, Zanzibar beckons with open arms, inviting you to explore its diverse tapestry.

CHAPTER 3

ACCOMMODATION

Welcome to the world of staying in Zanzibar, where finding the perfect place to rest is as exciting as the adventures that await you on this enchanting island. In this chapter, we'll navigate through the diverse options, from luxurious escapes to budget-friendly hideaways, ensuring your stay in Zanzibar is nothing short of extraordinary.

Types of Accommodations Available

Zanzibar offers a tapestry of accommodation options to cater to every traveler's taste and preferences.

- Hotels, Resorts, and Guesthouses

Hotels: These are like your home away from home but with a touch of luxury. They come in various sizes and styles, offering comfort and convenience.

Resorts: Imagine a place where relaxation meets indulgence. Resorts in Zanzibar often feature stunning amenities, from pools to spas, providing an all-encompassing experience.

Guesthouses: For a more intimate setting, guesthouses offer a chance to connect with the local culture. They are often family-run, providing a cozy and welcoming atmosphere.

- Unique Stays and Boutique Accommodations

Unique Stays: Think beyond traditional accommodations. Zanzibar has unique stays like treehouses, beach huts, and even historical homes turned into cozy retreats.

Boutique Accommodations: These are like hidden gems, small and stylish hotels that offer a personalized experience. Each room is carefully curated, creating a charming and intimate atmosphere.

During my stay in Zanzibar, I opted for a charming boutique guesthouse in Stone Town. Tucked away in the narrow lanes, it provided a blend of local culture and modern comfort. The personal touch in the service and unique decor made my stay memorable.

Top Hotels and Resorts

For those who seek a touch of luxury and the finest amenities, Zanzibar boasts some of the top hotels and resorts in the world.

- Luxury Accommodations

Luxury hotels in Zanzibar redefine opulence. From private villas to personalized services, these accommodations are designed to pamper and indulge.

- Exclusive Beachfront Resorts

If waking up to the sound of the ocean and feeling the sand beneath your feet is your dream, Zanzibar's exclusive beachfront resorts offer an unparalleled experience.

A stay at a luxurious beachfront resort in Nungwi elevated my Zanzibar experience. The panoramic views of the Indian Ocean, coupled with impeccable service, created a haven of relaxation.

Budget-Friendly Options

For the savvy traveler, Zanzibar presents budget-friendly options that allow you to enjoy the beauty of the island without breaking the bank.

- Hostels and Budget Hotels

Perfect for solo travelers or those seeking a communal atmosphere, hostels and budget hotels offer a wallet-friendly way to experience Zanzibar.

- Affordable Guesthouses

Immerse yourself in the local vibe by choosing an affordable guesthouse. These accommodations not only provide a cozy stay but also a chance to connect with the vibrant community.

Exploring Zanzibar on a budget led me to a quaint guest house in Paje. The laid-back atmosphere and interactions with fellow travelers created a sense of camaraderie.

Tips for Booking and Choosing Accommodation

Choosing the right place to stay is crucial for an enjoyable trip. Here are a few useful pointers to help you get started.

- Booking Platforms Comparison

With numerous booking platforms available, it's essential to compare prices, reviews, and amenities. Popular platforms like Booking.com, Airbnb, and Expedia can offer different perspectives on accommodations.

- Local Recommendations

Sometimes, the best advice comes from those who know the place well. Local recommendations from residents or fellow travelers can provide valuable insights into hidden gems and off-the-beaten-path accommodations.

Engaging with locals led me to discover a charming homestay in Jambiani, recommended by a friendly local. It turned out to be a hidden gem away from the tourist crowds.

Zanzibar's accommodation options are as diverse as the island itself. Whether you crave luxury, seek budget-friendly stays, or desire unique experiences, Zanzibar has the perfect place for you to call home during your adventure. As you plan your stay, consider your preferences, explore the diverse options, and get ready for a memorable journey in this tropical paradise.

CHAPTER 4

DINING AND CUISINE

Prepare your taste buds for a culinary journey through the flavors of Zanzibar, where each dish is a symphony of spices and every dining experience is a celebration of the island's vibrant culinary heritage.

Local Cuisine and Popular Dishes

- Spice-Infused Delicacies

Zanzibar's cuisine is a fusion of cultures, with a prominent influence of spices that have shaped its identity. Indulge in spice-infused delicacies like "Pilau," a fragrant rice dish cooked with a medley of spices, and "Biriani," a flavorful combination of rice, meat, and aromatic spices.

Savoring a plate of Pilau in a local eatery immersed me in the essence of Zanzibari spices. The harmonious blend of flavors, from cardamom to cinnamon, created a culinary symphony that left a lasting impression.

- Seafood Specialties

With its coastal location, Zanzibar boasts a seafood extravaganza. From grilled lobster to coconut-infused fish curries, the seafood specialties reflect the island's maritime charm. Don't miss trying "Urojo," a tangy seafood soup that captures the essence of Zanzibar's coastal culinary artistry.

Dining on the beach with a platter of grilled lobster, accompanied by the rhythmic sounds of the ocean, was a seafood indulgence like no other. The freshness of the catch and the coastal breeze added a touch of magic to the experience.

Best Restaurants

- Fine Dining Experiences

For those seeking refined culinary adventures, Zanzibar offers fine dining experiences that showcase the artistry of its chefs. From elegant seafood restaurants to intimate dining spaces, indulge in gourmet creations inspired by local ingredients.

- Local Favorites

Explore the hidden gems that locals cherish. These restaurants may not have Michelin stars, but they hold the heart of Zanzibar's culinary soul. Enjoy dishes that reflect the authenticity and warmth of Zanzibari home cooking.

A tucked-away eatery recommended by a local introduced me to a feast of flavors. The communal dining atmosphere and the genuine smiles of the staff created a sense of belonging.

Street Food and Local Eateries

- Must-Try Street Snacks

Take to the streets and explore the vibrant world of Zanzibar's street food. From "Zanzibar Mix," a local favorite featuring a blend of meats and spices, to "Mshikaki," succulent skewers of grilled meat, street snacks offer a quick and delicious taste of the island.

- Hidden Gems for Foodies

Beyond the popular tourist spots, Zanzibar hides culinary treasures waiting to be discovered. Venture into local eateries tucked in narrow alleys, where the aroma of spices and the sizzle of street grills beckon adventurous foodies.

Strolling through the Stone Town alleys led me to a tiny stall where a friendly vendor served up Mshikaki. The smoky aroma and the burst of flavors with each bite made it a culinary adventure worth savoring.

Dining by the Sea

- Beachside Restaurants

Enhance your dining experience by choosing beachside restaurants that offer stunning views of the Indian Ocean. Feel the sand beneath your feet as you relish seafood delights, creating memories against the backdrop of the picturesque Zanzibar coastline.

- Sunset Dinner Spots

As the sun paints the sky in hues of orange and pink, Zanzibar's sunset dinner spots become enchanting settings for a romantic or relaxed evening. Enjoy a meal as you watch the sun dip below the horizon, casting a golden glow over the island.

A sunset dinner on the shores of Paje, with the sky ablaze in colors, created a moment of serenity. The combination of nature's beauty and delectable cuisine was a sensory delight.

Local Wine Tasting Experiences

- Zanzibari Wine Culture

Explore the emerging wine culture of Zanzibar, where locally produced wines complement the island's cuisine. From fruity Maracuja wine to the robust flavors of banana wine, indulge in unique blends that reflect Zanzibar's diverse agricultural offerings.

- Unique Tasting Tours

Embark on tasting tours that introduce you to the art of Zanzibari winemaking. Visit local vineyards, meet passionate winemakers, and savor the distinct notes of each varietal, creating a sensory experience that complements the island's culinary scene.

A guided wine tour opened my palate to the nuances of Zanzibar's unique wines. Sampling the different varieties, each infused with local fruits, added a delightful twist to my gastronomic journey.

In summary, Zanzibar's dining and cuisine are a feast for the senses, offering a kaleidoscope of flavors that reflect the island's rich cultural tapestry. Whether indulging in spice-infused delicacies, savoring street food delights, or enjoying a romantic beachside dinner, Zanzibar's culinary scene is as diverse as the island itself. As you embark on this gastronomic adventure, let the flavors of Zanzibar tantalize your taste buds and create memories that linger long after the last bite.

CHAPTER 5

OUTDOOR ACTIVITIES AND ADVENTURE

Prepare to embrace the outdoor wonders of Zanzibar, where every step becomes an adventure and nature unfolds its treasures. In this chapter, we'll explore the diverse array of outdoor activities that make Zanzibar a paradise for thrill-seekers and nature enthusiasts alike.

Hiking Trails Galore

- Scenic Routes and Nature Walks

Zanzibar's landscape offers a tapestry of scenic beauty waiting to be explored. From the lush Jozani Chwaka Bay National Park to the rugged terrain of Ngezi Forest, embark on nature walks that reveal the island's diverse ecosystems and wildlife.

Venturing into Jozani Chwaka Bay National Park, the vibrant colors of butterflies and the rustle of monkeys in the treetops created a magical atmosphere. The guided nature walk provided insights into Zanzibar's unique biodiversity.

- Hiking Tips and Trails

For those seeking an elevated adventure, Zanzibar presents hiking trails that lead to breathtaking viewpoints. Whether climbing to the top of Pugu Hills or exploring the trails of Nungwi, heed practical hiking tips and embrace the natural wonders that unfold with each ascent.

Hiking to the summit of Pugu Hills offered panoramic views of the island. The sense of accomplishment, coupled with the stunning vistas, made it a rewarding outdoor experience.

Boat Tours and Water Adventures

- Snorkeling and Diving Spots

Explore the rich underwater world by taking a dive into the crystal-clear waters surrounding Zanzibar. Explore renowned snorkeling spots like Mnemba Atoll or dive into the depths of Chumbe Island Coral Park, where colorful coral reefs and marine life await.

Snorkeling off the shores of Mnemba Atoll introduced me to a kaleidoscope of coral and fish. The underwater tranquility and the dance of marine life made it an unforgettable aquatic adventure.

- Sailing Excursions

Set sail on the Indian Ocean and let the sea breeze carry you to secluded coves and pristine beaches. Join a sailing excursion to explore hidden gems like Prison Island or simply relax on the deck, soaking in the beauty of Zanzibar's coastline.

A sunset sailing excursion to Prison Island offered a unique perspective of Zanzibar's shores. The rhythmic sway of the boat and the golden hues of the setting sun created a serene maritime escape.

Cycling Through Zanzibar's Countryside

- Bike Rental Information

For those who prefer a leisurely pace, cycling through Zanzibar's countryside provides a delightful way to explore. Learn about bike rental options and set out on cycling routes that take you through spice plantations, quaint villages, and coastal trails.

Renting a bike and pedaling through the spice-scented air of rural Zanzibar was a rejuvenating experience. The freedom to explore at my own pace allowed me to uncover hidden gems off the beaten path.

- Cycling Routes

Discover the diverse landscapes of Zanzibar through recommended cycling routes. From the rolling hills of Kidike to the coastal roads of Jambiani, each route offers a unique perspective of the island's natural beauty.

Cycling through the scenic routes of Jambiani allowed me to witness the daily life of local communities. The gentle breeze and ever-changing landscapes made it a picturesque journey.

Beach Bliss

- Relaxing Beach Days

Zanzibar's beaches are not just for sunbathing; they are gateways to relaxation and rejuvenation. Whether you choose the lively shores of Kendwa or the tranquil beaches of Matemwe, bask in the tropical sun and let the sounds of the ocean serenade you.

Spending a lazy day on the powdery sands of Kendwa Beach, the gentle lapping of the waves and the warmth of the sun created a sense of pure bliss.

- Waterfront Activities

Dip your toes into a variety of waterfront activities, from paddleboarding in Nungwi to kayaking in Chwaka Bay. Embrace the dynamic energy of the ocean while enjoying water sports that cater to all skill levels.

Trying paddleboarding in Nungwi added an element of thrill to my beach day. The clear waters and the sense of floating above the ocean provided a unique perspective of the coastline.

Rock Climbing and Adventure Sports

- Thrilling Rock Climbing Spots

For adrenaline enthusiasts, Zanzibar offers rock climbing opportunities on the cliffs of Kidike or at Kichwele Forest Reserve. Scale the heights and enjoy panoramic views as a reward for conquering these natural rock formations.

Rock climbing in Kidike was an exhilarating challenge. The feeling of reaching the summit and the stunning views of the surrounding landscape made it a memorable outdoor adventure.

- Adventure Sports Opportunities

Beyond rock climbing, Zanzibar provides a playground for various adventure sports. From kitesurfing in Paje to quad biking in the countryside, indulge in activities that blend excitement with the natural beauty of the island.

Trying kitesurfing in the waters of Paje added an element of thrill to my Zanzibar adventure. The adrenaline rush and the mastery of harnessing the wind made it an unforgettable experience.

In conclusion, Zanzibar's outdoor activities and adventures invite you to explore the island's diverse landscapes, from lush forests to pristine beaches. Whether hiking through nature reserves, diving into the azure waters, or embracing the thrill of rock climbing, Zanzibar caters to every outdoor enthusiast. As you embark on these adventures, let the natural beauty of Zanzibar be your guide, leading you to unforgettable moments of exploration and discovery.

CHAPTER 6

ART, CULTURE, AND ENTERTAINMENT

Immerse yourself in the vibrant tapestry of Zanzibar's art, culture, and entertainment. In this chapter, we'll explore the island's rich heritage through local festivals, artistic showcases, shopping adventures, and the lively nightlife that adds rhythm to Zanzibar's evenings.

Local Festivals and Events

- Annual Cultural Celebrations

Zanzibar comes alive with a plethora of annual cultural celebrations that showcase the island's traditions. From the exuberant celebration of Sauti za Busara, a music festival in Stone Town, to the colorful spectacle of Mwaka Kogwa, a Swahili New Year's festival, delve into the cultural calendar that defines Zanzibar's festive spirit.

Attending Sauti za Busara was a sensory feast of music, dance, and vibrant colors. The fusion of traditional and contemporary sounds created an electric atmosphere that resonated with the soul of Zanzibar.

- Festival Calendar

Plan your visit around Zanzibar's festival calendar, ensuring you don't miss the island's dynamic events. Whether it's the Zanzibar International Film Festival or the celebration of the Zanzibar Revolution Day, each festival offers a unique perspective of the island's cultural diversity.

Being part of the Zanzibar International Film Festival allowed me to appreciate the island's emerging talent and the global influence of Zanzibari cinema.

Art Galleries and Museums

- Cultural Exhibits and Displays

Discover Zanzibar's artistic soul through visits to local art galleries and museums. From the vibrant displays at the Emerson on Hurumzi to the historical artifacts at the Palace Museum, explore the artistic and historical narratives that shape the island's identity.

Roaming through the rooms of the Emerson on Hurumzi, adorned with local artwork and historical artifacts, offered a glimpse into Zanzibar's cultural evolution.

- Must-Visit Art Spaces

Navigate the labyrinthine streets of Stone Town to uncover must-visit art spaces, from the Malindi Art Center to the Zanzibar Gallery. Each venue provides a platform for local artists to showcase their talents, creating a dynamic hub for artistic expression.

Stumbling upon the Malindi Art Center introduced me to the diverse expressions of Zanzibari artists. The intimate setting and the opportunity to interact with the creators added depth to my understanding of local art.

Shopping and Markets

- Souvenir Shopping Guide

Embark on a journey through Zanzibar's markets, where a treasure trove of souvenirs awaits. From intricately carved wooden crafts to vibrant fabrics at Darajani Market, this shopping guide ensures you bring home a piece of Zanzibar's artistic heritage.

Exploring the stalls of Darajani Market was a sensory overload. The vibrant colors, the fragrant spices, and the friendly banter with local vendors created a memorable shopping experience.

- Local Markets Exploration

Delve into the heart of local markets, where the pulse of Zanzibar's daily life beats. Join the bustling crowds at Forodhani Market for street food delights or navigate the narrow alleys of Mwanakwerekwe Market for a glimpse into the island's culinary and cultural offerings.

Forodhani Market, with its array of street food stalls, was a culinary adventure. Trying local delicacies and interacting with the vibrant market atmosphere added a flavorful dimension to my Zanzibar journey.

Nightlife and Entertainment Options

- Bars, Clubs, and Live Music

As the sun sets, Zanzibar transforms into a lively haven for nightlife enthusiasts. From the laid-back atmosphere of Red Monkey Lodge in Jambiani to the pulsating beats of Livingstone Beach Restaurant in Stone Town, explore the bars, clubs, and live music venues that keep the island awake.

The rhythmic beats at Livingstone Beach Restaurant created a dance-worthy ambiance. The blend of live music, ocean views, and the energy of fellow revelers made it a memorable night on the town.

- Evening Entertainment Recommendations

Unwind in the evenings with a selection of entertainment options, from traditional Taarab music performances to beachside bonfires. Discover the enchanting blend of cultural rhythms and contemporary beats that define Zanzibar's diverse entertainment scene.

Attending a Taarab music performance under the stars was a soulful experience. The melodic tunes and the cultural richness of the performance resonated with the island's deep-rooted traditions.

In summary, Zanzibar's art, culture, and entertainment beckon you into a world of vibrant festivals, artistic expressions, and lively evenings. Whether immersing yourself in the beats of a music festival, exploring local art galleries, indulging in a shopping spree, or dancing the night away, Zanzibar ensures every moment is infused with the island's unique cultural charm. As you navigate this chapter, let the rhythm of Zanzibar guide your exploration of its artistic and entertaining soul, creating memories that echo the lively spirit of the island.

CHAPTER 7

7-DAY ITINERARY

Embark on a carefully crafted 7-day journey through Zanzibar, where each day unfolds a new facet of the island's beauty and charm. Whether you're a culture enthusiast, nature lover, or beach bum, this itinerary is designed to immerse you in the diverse experiences that Zanzibar has to offer.

Day 1:

Arrival Details and Exploration of Stone Town

- Morning: Arrival and Check-In

Arrive in Zanzibar and seamlessly transition into the island's laid-back rhythm. Check-in to your chosen accommodation and refresh yourself for the adventures ahead.

Arriving in Zanzibar, the warm hospitality of the staff at my chosen accommodation set the tone for a relaxing stay.

- Afternoon: Stone Town Walking Tour

Embark on a walking tour of Stone Town, a UNESCO World Heritage site. Lose yourself in the labyrinthine alleys, where each weathered door and bustling market tells tales of a bygone era.

Wandering through the narrow streets of Stone Town, I felt like a time traveler. The architecture and vibrant markets brought history to life.

- Evening: Sunset Dinner by the Sea

As the day winds down, savor a sunset dinner by the sea. Choose a beachside restaurant and let the soothing sound of the waves complement the delectable local cuisine.

The hues of the setting sun and the sound of the ocean provided a perfect backdrop for a memorable dinner by the sea.

Day 2:

Spice Plantations and Jozani Chwaka Bay National Park

- Morning: Spice Tour

Take a spice tour and go on a sensory adventure. Explore the lush spice plantations, learning about Zanzibar's historic connection to the spice trade.

The aroma of cloves, cardamom, and cinnamon enveloped me during the spice tour, creating a captivating olfactory experience.

- Afternoon: Jozani Forest Exploration

Head to Jozani Chwaka Bay National Park for an afternoon in the heart of nature. Discover the unique flora and fauna, including the rare red colobus monkeys.

Spotting the playful red colobus monkeys in Jozani Forest was a highlight, showcasing the biodiversity of Zanzibar.

- Evening: Cultural Dinner Experience

Immerse yourself in Zanzibar's cultural richness with a traditional dinner experience. Enjoy local dishes accompanied by traditional music and dance.

The cultural dinner provided a taste of authentic Zanzibari hospitality, with the rhythmic beats of traditional music creating a festive atmosphere.

Day 3:

Beach Day and Water Adventures

- Morning: Relaxing at the Beach

Indulge in a leisurely morning at one of Zanzibar's pristine beaches. Feel the soft sand between your toes as you soak in the tropical sun.

Lounging on the powdery sands of Nungwi Beach, I relished the serenity and the panoramic views of the turquoise waters.

- Afternoon: Snorkeling Excursion

Take a snorkelling trip to discover the wonders beneath the surface. Dive into the clear waters and witness the vibrant marine life.

Snorkeling off the shores of Mnemba Atoll introduced me to a kaleidoscope of coral and fish, creating an aquatic adventure.

- Evening: Beachside BBQ

As the sun sets, enjoy a beachside barbecue. Savor grilled seafood and local specialties while listening to the gentle lapping of the waves.

The beachside barbecue under the stars was a delightful culinary experience, blending the flavors of the sea with the ambiance of the beach.

Day 4:

Historical Exploration - Old Fort and House of Wonders

- Morning: Old Fort Visit

Embark on a historical journey with a visit to the Old Fort. Explore the architectural marvel and learn about its significance in Zanzibar's history.

The Old Fort's imposing structure and historical significance provided a glimpse into Zanzibar's past as a maritime powerhouse.

- Afternoon: House of Wonders Tour

Discover the House of Wonders, a symbol of Zanzibar's cultural heritage. Explore the exhibits and artifacts that showcase the island's rich history.

Walking through the halls of the House of Wonders, I marveled at the intricate displays that encapsulated Zanzibar's cultural evolution.

- Evening: Local Cuisine Dinner

Wrap up the day with a dinner featuring local cuisine. Choose a restaurant in Stone Town to experience the authentic flavors of Zanzibari dishes.

The local cuisine dinner was a gastronomic delight, with flavors that reflected the island's cultural influences.

Day 5:

Nature Walks and Local Villages

- Morning: Nature Walk

Embark on a nature walk to explore the scenic landscapes of Zanzibar. Choose a trail that takes you through lush forests or along the coastline.

The nature walk provided a tranquil escape, allowing me to connect with Zanzibar's natural beauty and diverse ecosystems.

- Afternoon: Visit to Local Villages

Immerse yourself in the local culture with a visit to nearby villages. Interact with residents, learn about their way of life, and gain insights into Zanzibar's community spirit.

Exploring local villages offered a genuine cultural exchange, providing a glimpse into the daily lives of Zanzibar's friendly residents.

- Evening: Sunset Drinks

Relax in the evening with drinks at a scenic spot. Whether on the beach or a rooftop terrace, savor the colors of the sunset with your favorite beverage.

Enjoying sunset drinks while overlooking the Indian Ocean added a touch of romance to the day, creating a serene and memorable moment.

Day 6:

Relaxing Beach Day

- Morning to Evening: Leisure Day at the Beach

Spend a day of leisure at one of Zanzibar's beautiful beaches. Relax, read a book, or take a dip in the refreshing waters.

The leisure day at Paje Beach allowed me to unwind, offering a perfect balance of tranquility and the vibrant energy of the ocean.

- Optional Water Activities

For those seeking adventure, engage in optional water activities. From kite surfing to paddleboarding, there are options for every water enthusiast.

Trying paddleboarding added an element of thrill to my beach day, providing a new perspective of the coastline.

Day 7:

Departure Preparations

- Morning: Last-Minute Explorations

Make the most of your final morning with some last-minute explorations. Visit any remaining attractions or simply stroll through the charming streets of Stone Town.

The last-minute explorations allowed me to revisit favorite spots and bid farewell to the iconic landmarks of Zanzibar.

- Afternoon: Check-Out and Departure

As you get ready to go, check out of your lodging. Ensure you have all your belongings and travel documents in order.

Checking out was seamless, with the attentive staff ensuring a hassle-free departure and leaving me with fond memories of Zanzibar.

- Evening: Farewell Dinner

Conclude your Zanzibar adventure with a farewell dinner. Choose a restaurant with a view to savor your last moments on the island.

The farewell dinner, with its blend of delicious cuisine and a view of the twinkling stars, provided a fitting conclusion to my unforgettable week in Zanzibar.

In conclusion, this 7-day itinerary is a curated journey that captures the essence of Zanzibar's beauty, from its historical sites to its pristine beaches. As you follow the daily activities and create your own memories, may this itinerary serve as a guide to a transformative and enriching experience on the enchanting island of Zanzibar.

CHAPTER 8

PRACTICAL INFORMATION AND TIPS

Prepare for a seamless exploration of Zanzibar with essential practical information and valuable tips. This chapter is your go-to guide for navigating cultural nuances, ensuring safety, and optimizing your communication and connectivity throughout the journey.

Etiquette and Customs

- Cultural Respect Guidelines

Respect for local customs is integral to a positive travel experience in Zanzibar. Familiarize yourself with guidelines such as dressing modestly, particularly in rural areas and during religious occasions. Greetings are significant, with a handshake and a warm "Jambo" or "Habari" being common.

Embracing local greetings helped me connect with Zanzibari residents, creating an immediate sense of warmth and hospitality.

- Local Customs Awareness

Understand and appreciate local customs, including the significance of traditional attire and practices. For instance, removing your shoes before entering someone's home is a common gesture of respect. Engaging in conversations about local customs with residents provides valuable insights.

Participating in traditional customs, like sharing a cup of spiced tea, allowed me to connect with locals and gain a deeper understanding of their way of life.

Language and Communication

- Basic Communication Tips

While Swahili is the primary language, English is widely spoken in tourist areas. Learning a few basic Swahili phrases, such as "Asante" for thank you and "Karibu" for welcome, enhances your interactions. Non-verbal communication, like hand gestures, is also effective.

Attempting basic Swahili phrases elicited smiles and appreciation, breaking down language barriers and fostering a sense of camaraderie.

- Language Phrases for Travelers

Equip yourself with a handy list of language phrases for various situations, from greetings to asking for directions. This not only facilitates smoother communication but also demonstrates your respect for the local culture.

Learning a few phrases helped me navigate markets, engage with locals, and express gratitude in a culturally sensitive manner.

Health and Safety Tips

- Medical Services Information

Become familiar with where pharmacies and medical facilities are located. It is essential to have any necessary prescriptions along with a basic first aid kit on hand. Stay hydrated, especially in the tropical climate, and be mindful of local health recommendations.

A minor ailment prompted a visit to a local clinic, where the attentive medical staff provided prompt and effective care.

- Safety Precautions

Zanzibar is generally safe, but like any destination, it's essential to be vigilant. Avoid displaying valuables in crowded areas, be cautious at night, and use reputable transportation services. Stay informed about local customs to avoid unintentional breaches.

Adhering to safety guidelines allowed me to explore with confidence, appreciating the warm hospitality without compromising my well-being.

Emergency Contacts

- Local Emergency Numbers

Save local emergency numbers, including those for medical assistance and the police, on your phone. Additionally, have contact information for your country's consulate in case of emergencies.

Knowing local emergency numbers proved invaluable during a minor incident, ensuring swift assistance.

- Consulate Information

Locate your country's consulate in Zanzibar. They can provide assistance in case of lost documents, emergencies, or other unforeseen circumstances.

A visit to the consulate for a document-related matter showcased the diplomatic support available to travelers.

Communication and Internet Access

- SIM Card and Internet Options

Consider purchasing a local SIM card for cost-effective communication. Numerous providers offer affordable data plans, ensuring you stay connected. Additionally, explore Wi-Fi availability at accommodations and public spaces.

A local SIM card provided seamless connectivity, allowing me to navigate using maps, stay in touch, and share my experiences in real-time.

- Wi-Fi Availability

Check for Wi-Fi availability at your accommodation and popular tourist spots. This ensures you can stay connected, share your experiences, and access essential information.

Reliable Wi-Fi at accommodations allowed me to plan activities, stay in touch with loved ones, and share travel moments effortlessly.

Useful Apps, Websites, and Maps

- Travel Apps Recommendations

Explore travel apps tailored for Zanzibar, offering insights into local attractions, transportation options, and cultural events. Apps like currency converters and language translators can also enhance your experience.

Using travel apps streamlined my itinerary, helping me discover hidden gems and access real-time information.

- Online Maps and Guides

Access online maps and guides for Zanzibar to navigate the island efficiently. Whether exploring Stone Town or embarking on outdoor adventures, having digital maps at your fingertips is invaluable.

Online maps facilitated solo exploration, allowing me to navigate the labyrinthine streets of Stone Town and discover off-the-beaten-path locations.

In conclusion, arming yourself with practical information and tips ensures a smooth and enjoyable exploration of Zanzibar. From respecting local customs to prioritizing health and safety, this chapter equips you with the knowledge to navigate the island with confidence. As you immerse yourself in the unique experiences Zanzibar offers, may these practical insights enhance the richness of your journey.

CONCLUSION

UNVEILING ZANZIBAR'S MAGICAL JOURNEY

As we reach the culmination of our expedition through the sun-kissed shores, historical wonders, and cultural treasures of Zanzibar, let us pause and reflect on the tapestry of experiences woven into the very fabric of this captivating destination. Our journey has been a symphony of flavors, a dance with history, and a communion with the warm embrace of Zanzibar's enchanting spirit.

A Tapestry of Cultural Riches

From the labyrinthine alleys of Stone Town to the vibrant hues of local festivals, Zanzibar has opened its arms wide to share its cultural riches. The echoes of traditional music, the aromas of spice-laden markets, and the genuine warmth of the locals have left an indelible mark on our hearts. In our exploration of local customs and engagement with Zanzibar's communities, we discovered that travel is not merely about witnessing, but actively participating in the rich tapestry of cultures.

Nature's Bounty Unveiled

Nature, in all its resplendent glory, has been our companion throughout this journey. From the pristine beaches that cradle the turquoise waters to the lush interiors adorned with spice plantations, Zanzibar showcases the wonders of the natural world. The red colobus monkeys of Jozani Forest and the vibrant coral gardens beneath the ocean waves have reminded us of the delicate balance between humanity and the environment. Our time spent on nature walks, beach excursions, and outdoor adventures has underscored the importance of preserving the beauty that Zanzibar so graciously shares with us.

Historical Marvels and Architectural Gems

Zanzibar's history is etched in the stone walls of Stone Town and the corridors of ancient forts. As we wandered through the historical sites, we were transported through time, witnessing the tales of Swahili sultans, Arabian traders, and European explorers. The Old Fort and the House of Wonders stand as silent witnesses to the maritime prowess and cultural legacy of this island. Our exploration of these historical marvels has ignited a deeper appreciation for the enduring spirit that resides within the very foundations of Zanzibar.

A Gastronomic Odyssey

The culinary journey through Zanzibar has been a feast for the senses, with every bite unveiling the rich tapestry of flavors that define this island. From spice-infused delicacies to seafood extravaganzas, the local cuisine is a testament to the island's historical connections and vibrant culture. Our exploration of dining by the sea, street food delights, and local wine tasting experiences has been a celebration of Zanzibar's culinary heritage. In savoring these gastronomic delights, we have not only satisfied our palates but also embraced the essence of Zanzibar's cultural fusion.

Adventure Beyond Boundaries

Zanzibar is not merely a destination; it's an adventure waiting to unfold. The hiking trails that wind through lush landscapes, the boat tours that reveal hidden coves, and the thrill of rock climbing against the backdrop of the Indian Ocean have beckoned us to step out of our comfort zones. Our cycling escapades through the countryside and blissful beach days have reminded us that true adventure lies in the willingness to explore the unknown. Zanzibar, with its myriad of outdoor activities, invites us to be adventurers in our own stories.

A Symphony of Arts, Culture, and Entertainment

The vibrancy of Zanzibar extends beyond its landscapes and into the heart of its arts, culture, and entertainment scene. Local festivals and events, art galleries, museums, and the pulsating nightlife have unveiled the dynamic spirit that defines Zanzibar. Our participation in these cultural celebrations and exploration of artistic expressions has underscored the role of creativity in shaping the identity of a place. Zanzibar, with its kaleidoscope of cultural offerings, has encouraged us to embrace the arts as an integral part of our travels.

A 7-Day Itinerary: A Blueprint for Immersive Exploration

Our 7-day itinerary has been more than a guide; it's a roadmap for a transformative odyssey. From the bustling arrival in Stone Town to the leisurely beach days and the historical explorations, each day has been a chapter in the unfolding story of Zanzibar. As we revisited our experiences in crafting this itinerary, the underlying message became clear: Zanzibar invites us not only to witness its beauty but to immerse ourselves fully in its diverse offerings.

Practical Wisdom for the Journey

Arming ourselves with practical wisdom has been instrumental in navigating the intricacies of Zanzibar. From understanding local etiquette and customs to embracing linguistic nuances, we've fostered meaningful connections. Our commitment to health and safety, coupled with insights into emergency contacts, has empowered us to explore with confidence. The seamless communication facilitated by local SIM cards and the convenience of online maps and travel apps have been our allies in unlocking the secrets of Zanzibar.

A Journey Beyond the Pages

As we close the chapters of this Zanzibar travel guide, let it be not the end but a beginning—a beginning of countless stories waiting to be written. Zanzibar, with its magical allure, has invited us to transcend the boundaries of a conventional trip and embark on a personal odyssey. The essence of Zanzibar lies not just in its landscapes but in the connections we've forged, the cultures we've embraced, and the stories we've collected along the way.

Your Zanzibar Adventure Awaits

As you hold the essence of Zanzibar in your hands, let it be more than a book; let it be a key to unlock your own extraordinary adventure. The call to action is not just to read about Zanzibar but to experience it—to savor the flavors, feel the rhythms, and create your own narrative on this enchanting island. Beyond these pages lies the promise of a transformative journey that transcends the ordinary.

In the Spirit of Zanzibar, Embrace the Extraordinary

Zanzibar is more than a destination; it's an invitation to embrace the extraordinary. It's an affirmation that travel is not just about reaching a place but about immersing oneself in its soul. As you embark on your Zanzibar odyssey, remember that the magic is not confined to the glossy pages of this guide; it's waiting to unfold with every step you take, every conversation you engage in, and every discovery you make.

May Your Zanzibar Story Begin Now

In the spirit of Zanzibar's warm hospitality, I extend my heartfelt gratitude for joining me on this journey. May your Zanzibar story begin now—an unwritten chapter awaiting the magic of your footsteps and the curiosity of your heart. Let this conclusion not be an end but a commencement, and as you step into the world that Zanzibar has unveiled, may it be a world where the extraordinary becomes your ordinary.

Safe travels, fellow adventurers. Your Zanzibar odyssey awaits.